D1362386

DATE DUE	
JUL 1 9 2007	
NOV 2 1 2008	
JUL 2 2009	
JUL 2 2 2011	
GAYLORD	PRINTED IN U.S.A.

CRAWSHAW PAINTS ACRYLICS

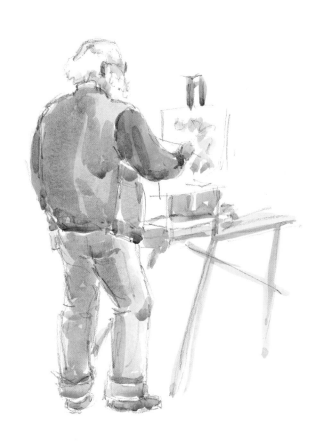

ALWYN CRAWSHAW

HarperCollins*Publishers*

in association with
Channel Four Television Corporation
and J. R. Productions

First published in 1994 by
HarperCollins Publishers, London

© Alwyn Crawshaw, 1994

Edited and typeset by Flicka Lister
Designer: Susan Howe

Photography: Nigel Cheffers-Heard
Location photography: Liam Furlong

Alwyn Crawshaw asserts the moral right to be
identified as the author of this work.

**A catalogue record for this book is available
from the British Library**

ISBN 0 00 412761 7
Printed and bound in the UK

ACKNOWLEDGEMENTS

June and I would like to express our grateful
thanks to all the members of the television film
crew for their tremendous support during the
making of *Crawshaw Paints Acrylics* – in
particular to our producer, David John Hare,
and also Scotty, our chief cameraman, for his
patience and delightful sense of humour.

We would also like to record our sincere
thanks to Cathy Gosling from HarperCollins,
to Flicka Lister for editing this book, and also to
Mary Poole for typing the manuscript.

June and I would like to express our gratitude
to all the wonderful people of Ireland for their
warmth and hospitality during our stay.

Finally, we would also like to thank the
following companies for their valuable
assistance in making the television series:

Irish Tourist Board
Aer Lingus
Swansea Cork Ferries
Great Southern Hotel, Parknasilla
Derrynane Hotel, Caherdaniel
Daihatsu UK
Canon UK
Air SouthWest

The eight-part television series, *Crawshaw Paints
Acrylics*, was produced and directed by
David John Hare for Channel 4. Videos of the
series are available from Teaching Art Ltd,
P O Box 50, Newark, Notts NG23 5GY;
telephone 0400 281492.

For further information about travel to and
accommodation in the Ring of Kerry, and for
more details about the locations in the television
series, please contact Teaching Art Ltd for a full
fact sheet.

All the close-up details in this book have been
enlarged by 25 per cent to show the way in which
the brush strokes have been formed. The sketches on
cartridge paper were done using a 2B pencil.

CONTENTS

ABOUT THE ARTISTS

ALWYN CRAWSHAW

Successful painter, author and teacher Alwyn Crawshaw was born at Mirfield, Yorkshire, and studied at Hastings School of Art. He now lives in Dawlish, Devon, with his wife June, where they have their own gallery.

As well as painting in acrylics, Alwyn also works in oils, watercolour and occasionally pastels. He is a fellow of the Royal Society of Arts, and a member of the Society of Equestrian Artists and the British Watercolour Society. Alwyn is also President of The National Acrylic Painters Association.

Alwyn's best-selling book *A Brush with Art* accompanied his first 12-part Channel Four television series in 1991, followed by *Crawshaw Paints on Holiday*, *Crawshaw Paints Oils* and *Crawshaw's Watercolour Studio*, all with tie-in books of the same titles. This book, *Crawshaw Paints Acrylics*, accompanies his fifth 8-part Channel Four television series.

Alwyn's books for HarperCollins include eight in their *Learn to Paint* series, *The Artist at Work* (an autobiography of his painting career), *Sketching with Alwyn Crawshaw*, *The Half-Hour Painter*, *Alwyn Crawshaw's Watercolour Painting Course*, *Alwyn Crawshaw's Oil Painting Course* and *Alwyn Crawshaw's Acrylic Painting Course*.

Alwyn has been a guest on local and national radio programmes, including *The Gay Byrne Radio Show* in Eire, and has appeared on various television programmes. Alwyn has made several successful videos on painting and in 1991 was listed as one of the top ten artist video teachers in America. He is also a regular contributor to *Leisure Painter* magazine.

Alwyn organizes his own successful and very popular painting courses and holidays, as well as giving demonstrations and lectures to art groups and societies throughout Britain. In 1992, he co-founded the Society of Amateur Artists, of which he is President. Alwyn has exhibited at the Royal Society of British Artists in London and he is listed in the current edition of *Who's Who in Art*.

Painted mainly from nature and still life, Alwyn's work has been favourably reviewed by critics. *The Telegraph Weekend Magazine* reported him to be 'a landscape painter of considerable expertise' and *The Artist's and Illustrator's Magazine* described him as 'outspoken about the importance of maintaining traditional values in the teaching of art.'

JUNE CRAWSHAW

Surrey-born June Crawshaw started her artistic career mainly as a potter. From 1980, she concentrated her creative talents on painting and continued to develop her own individual style of watercolour painting, retaining the same delicacy of touch and feel for beauty as her ceramics.

June now paints in watercolour, acrylics and oils. She is a member of the Society of Women Artists and a member of the British Watercolour Society. June is also listed in the current edition of *Who's·Who in Art*.

For the last ten years, June has taught with Alwyn on his residential painting courses, as well as painting alongside Alwyn in his previous television series *Crawshaw Paints on Holiday*. Her work is included in the tie-in book of the same title. June has just completed her first book, *Watercolour Made Easy*, to be published by HarperCollins in 1995.

Original work by June may be found in collections throughout this country and abroad. She exhibits her work in galleries in the UK and also at The Crawshaw Gallery in Dawlish.

INTRODUCTION

Painting the first picture for the television series

As I write this introduction, a haunting Irish melody is playing in the background on my stereo. It brings back wonderful memories of the time my wife June and I spent in County Kerry in southern Ireland, while filming *Crawshaw Paints Acrylics*, our fifth television series. In the series and this accompanying book, June and I show you how to work in acrylic colours as we paint the beautiful scenery in the Ring of Kerry.

PAINTING OUTSIDE

Before leaving for Ireland, June and I went to local painting spots to practise working with acrylic colours outdoors. It is unusual for either of us to paint outside in acrylics, simply because oil and watercolour are more practical for outdoor work. So, this was a challenge. The equipment normally needed for painting in acrylics isn't quite as easy to carry, or work with, as that used for the other two mediums, especially if you compare it to watercolour equipment. Also, acrylic paint dries very quickly on the canvas, especially in hot or windy climates, so it isn't necessarily the easiest option for working outdoors. However, as long as you are aware of the problems, there are ways of overcoming them and I wanted to demonstrate that, with a little forethought, acrylic paint can be used outside as comfortably as any other painting medium.

There are some important procedures to follow, however. When painting in acrylics, you must make sure your palette doesn't dry out while you are working, by using a Stay-Wet Palette (see page 13). When you are totally involved with your painting this can happen – it has to me. Also, setting up a palette can be frustrating, especially if it is windy!

If you are a flamboyant wielder of the brush, it is advisable to wear clothing that you don't mind getting paint on. Remember, once it has dried, you can't get acrylic paint off! If you do get paint on your clothes, put tissues underneath the area to stop the colour spreading, then apply plenty of water and sponge it off. I take a chance but June puts on an old painting shirt when she works.

Working outdoors with acrylics does have one practical advantage over oil paint. Because the paint dries quickly, an acrylic painting is always dry when you carry it on to your next painting spot or take it home.

Once I have got everything set up outside (which takes much longer than for watercolour and a little longer than for oil) I love working with acrylics. If you use a small pochade box rather than an easel, your setting-up time is minimal and it is a fabulous medium for sketching. On page 91 (top) in the Gallery you can see a delicate sketch I did during pre-filming 'practice' days, using my pochade box.

DIFFERENT TECHNIQUES

For each programme in the series, June and I used a different technique or chose different subjects to paint in order to demonstrate the versatility of this exciting medium. If you haven't painted in acrylics before, I suggest you work indoors to begin with. If you already paint in watercolour, start by using acrylics thinly and gradually build thicker and opaque colours over. This will lead you naturally into using acrylic colours to their maximum potential.

If you paint in oils, start by working as you would with oil colours. You will soon discover that you can work much more quickly over the top of previous painted areas, because of the quick drying time. Naturally you will find other differences. Experiment and practise and you will soon learn how versatile acrylic paint is.

Here June was totally involved with her painting

PRACTICE MAKES PERFECT

I often say 'have a go – it's easier than you think'. Then I usually continue by saying, 'but you must practise'. For instance, if I haven't done any pencil sketching for a while, I try to find time to practise, even if it's for just half an hour. In fact, when we flew to Ireland from Exeter Airport, I hadn't done any pencil sketching for a few weeks. This always concerns me because you can build up a mental barrier and think you have lost some of your skills.

We flew in a small eight-seater aircraft and, in cloud high over the Irish Sea, there was nothing to do. So I sketched the pilot and co-pilot with 2B pencil on cartridge paper. My pencil sketch is shown below. It took me about twenty minutes and when I had finished I was very pleased with myself because I had broken through that mental barrier and proved to myself that I could still use a pencil! Perhaps I have exaggerated the point, but only a little. Remember, the more you practise the more confident you will become and therefore you will paint better pictures.

This pencil sketch was done flying high over the Irish Sea on our way to Kerry

THE TELEVISION SERIES

During our stay in Ireland, although we had some gloriously sunny days, we also encountered our fair share of rain. Because of this, we had to make two television programmes indoors which were fairly complicated to film. However, they also were great fun to do, so the rain actually did us a favour!

In the first of these, I painted flowers and June painted a picture of me as I worked, and in the second we took our painting materials to The Blue Bull bar in the village of Sneem, where June and I thoroughly enjoyed capturing the atmosphere and hospitality of an Irish pub.

This was just one of the wonderful places we visited in this part of Ireland and the map below shows County Kerry and the locations where we painted the pictures for each programme in the television series.

June and I had a fabulous time while we were there and I hope this book inspires you to paint in acrylics, just as the gorgeous Irish scenery inspired us. Perhaps one day you will have the chance to follow and paint in our footsteps!

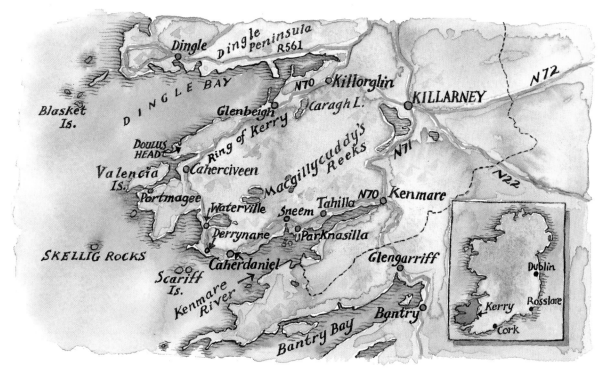

Follow our painting journey with this map of County Kerry

MATERIALS

Each artist's choice of materials is, of course, a very personal matter and, when you have gained experience, you will be ready to make your own decisions. In the meantime, if you are a beginner to acrylics, I suggest you use what I use. In order to get the best results, you should always use the best quality materials you can afford.

COLOURS

The acrylic colours I used for the television series are shown on the opposite page. These are all Daler-Rowney Artists' Cryla Flow Colours, which have a creamy consistency and come in tubes. Daler-Rowney also make another type of acrylic paint called Cryla Colour, which is thicker and has a more buttery consistency than Cryla Flow Colour – when you're shopping for colours, don't get the two confused!

Cryla Colour is ideal for work with a palette knife but can also be used with a brush and I love using it to add more texture to my paintings. But I didn't use it in the television series. If you haven't used acrylic colour before, my advice is to start painting with Cryla Flow Colours until you have more experience, then try the thicker paint and see if you gain anything extra from it.

I normally use the first eight colours shown on the opposite page and from these I can mix all the colours I require. However, there are exceptions to every rule and for the flower painting on page 40, I also used Cadmium Yellow Pale and Hooker's Green. June normally works in the same colours as me, although she uses Yellow Ochre in preference to Raw Sienna, and for the three primary colour painting on page 33 she used Cadmium Red, Cadmium Yellow Pale and Coeruleum for her blue.

BRUSHES

The range of brushes available for acrylic painting is vast. You can use most traditional oil painting brushes – these are made from hog bristle and come in various sizes with different shapes of bristle. You can also use synthetic (Dalon) and sable brushes. Obviously, as you gain experience, you will want to experiment with different types of brushes but, to get started, I suggest you choose from the ones I use. (See Basic Kit for brush sizes.)

Bristle brushes: Daler-Rowney's Bristlewhite Series B36.
Synthetic brushes: Daler-Rowney's Cryla Series C25, which is made specially for acrylic painting, and a Dalon Series D99 'Rigger' (the same brush I use for small detail in my watercolour painting).
Sable brush: I use my small watercolour brush.

From left to right, tubes of Cryla Flow Colour and Cryla Colour

THE ACRYLIC COLOURS USED IN THIS BOOK

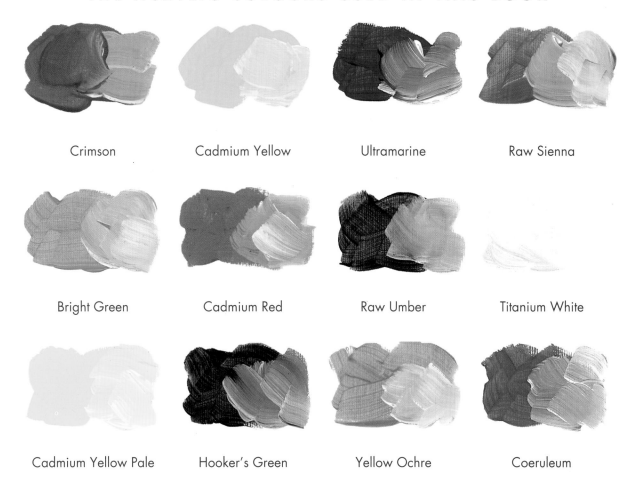

| Crimson | Cadmium Yellow | Ultramarine | Raw Sienna |

| Bright Green | Cadmium Red | Raw Umber | Titanium White |

| Cadmium Yellow Pale | Hooker's Green | Yellow Ochre | Coeruleum |

PAINTING SURFACES

There are many painting surfaces (grounds) on which to work. Make sure that the surface is free from oil or grease, and if the surface is too absorbent for you, then prime it with an acrylic primer (gesso). If you use an oil-primed canvas, always over-prime it with an acrylic primer.

When June or I used a watercolour technique on television, we worked on either cartridge paper, Bockingford or Waterford watercolour paper. For normal acrylic work, we used either Cryla Primed Paper (made specially for acrylic painting) or Waterford watercolour paper primed with two coats of acrylic primer. In Programme 7 (page 76) I painted on brown wrapping paper! All painting surfaces are given in captions throughout the book.

PALETTE

I can only recommend one palette and this is the Daler-Rowney Stay-Wet Palette. If you follow the instructions, your paints will keep wet almost indefinitely and it will save you a lot of paint!

EASEL

In the television series, I used the Daler-Rowney 'Salisbury' folding sketch box easel (shown on the front cover of the book) for larger work. It folds up like a small slim suitcase with a handle and carries all you need. I made a small plywood tray to put the water container on and rested my Stay-Wet palette on the front drawer of the easel. I found it very comfortable for acrylic painting.

TRAVELLING STUDIO

The self-contained pochade box of my Acrylic Travelling Studio, shown below, is similar to that of my Oil Travelling Studio and perfect for outside work. The oil palette has been removed and replaced with a Stay-Wet Palette. The colours are kept in the box with a pencil and brushes and I cut the brush handles shorter to fit the box. It has a leather strap to support it round your neck to enable you to work standing up if needed. This also acts as a shoulder strap for carrying. It contains two painting boards 15 x 20 cm (6 x 8 in) which slot into the lid.

In fact, the only item you need to carry separately is water for working with and cleaning your brushes!

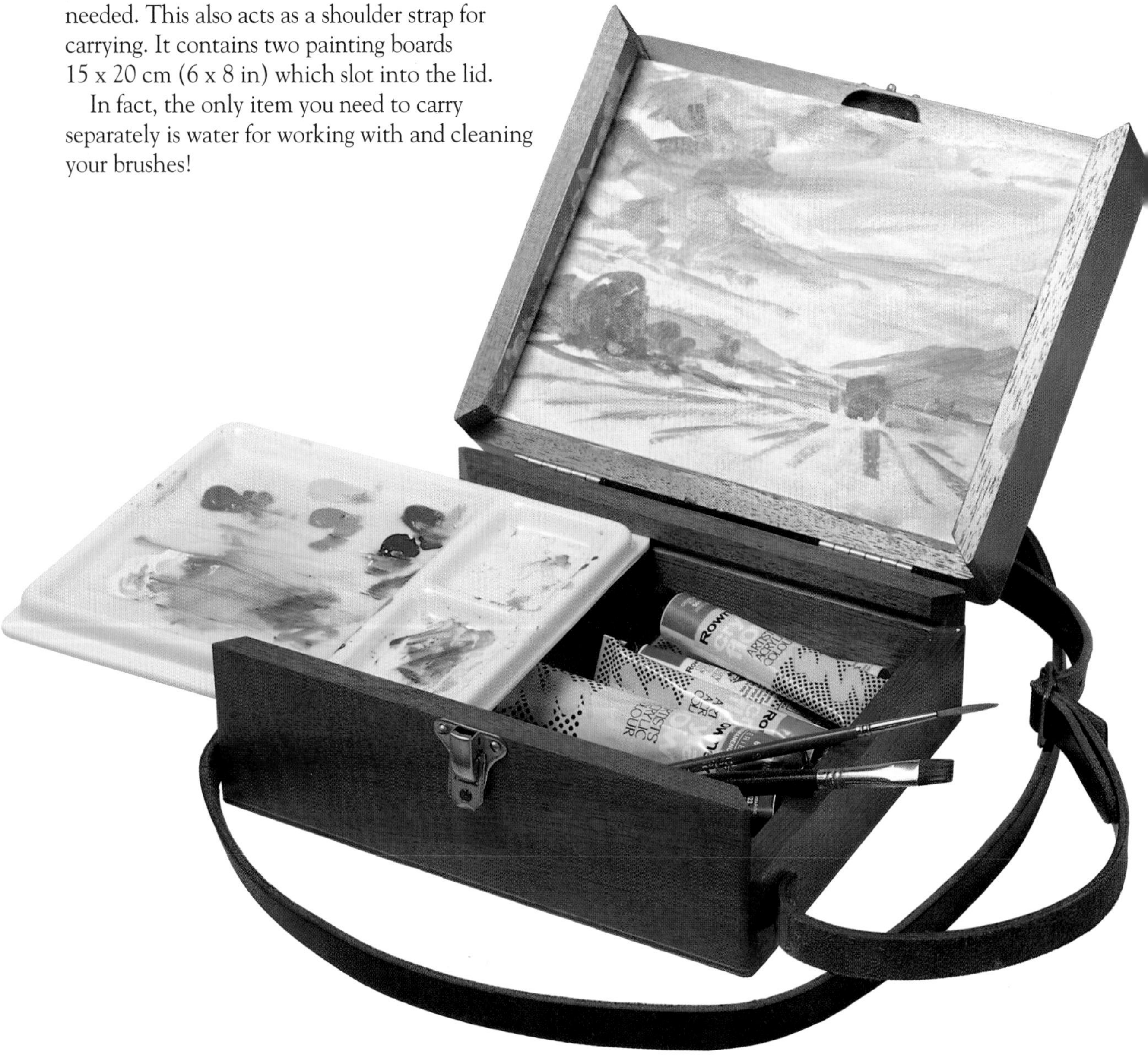

The Acrylic Travelling Studio

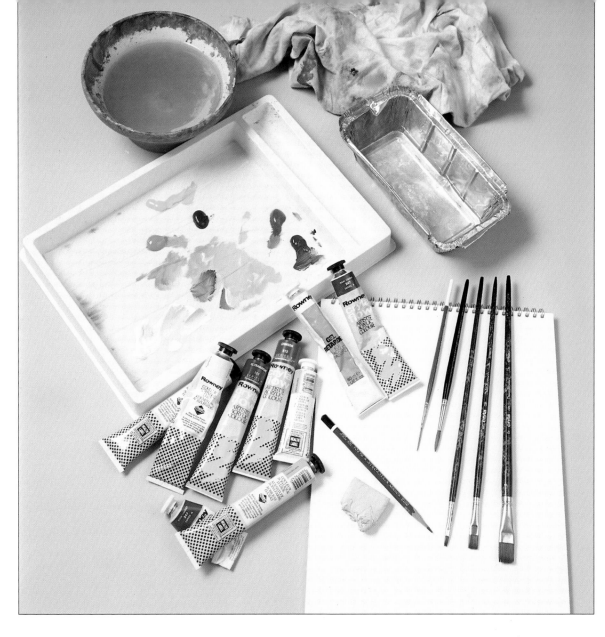

My basic acrylic kit

BASIC KIT

The picture above shows you the materials you will need to start painting in acrylic. I used the easel shown on the front cover for most of my painting in the series but to practise indoors you can rest your work against the back of a kitchen chair, or buy a small table easel. If you work on acrylic primed paper rather than expensive canvas, you won't need acrylic primer. My basic kit is only a guide, so you should always feel free to add materials of your choice. However, remember that the fewer materials you work with, the easier it will be for you to learn to paint

in acrylic! The colours you will need are the ones recommended on page 13. Your brushes should be either the Bristlewhite Series B36 Nos. 8, 4 and 2 or the Cryla Series C25 Nos. 12, 8, 4 and 2 plus a Dalon Series D99 'Rigger' No. 2, and a round sable No. 6.

You will need a Stay-Wet Palette and a Cryla sketchbook or a support of your choice; a pencil; plastic eraser; some rag; a water jar; a brush dish and a tube of Gel Retarder. When mixed with paint, this helps to slow down the drying time of paint on canvas (if you feel it is necessary). I only use Gel Retarder for large sky areas when I am working wet-on-wet paint.

THE 8 PROGRAMMES

1

ABOUT ACRYLICS

2

SCALE AND COLOUR

5

SKETCHING OUTSIDE

6

COMPARING MEDIUMS

A course of easy-to-follow acrylic painting lessons to accompany the television series

3

FLOWERS AND FIGURES

4

PANORAMIC LANDSCAPE

7

PAINTING PEOPLE

8

SIMPLIFYING A SCENE

ABOUT ACRYLICS

Acrylic colour has been available for the past thirty years and, compared to oil paint and watercolour, it is a relatively new medium. Unlike oil paint, you mix acrylic paint with water – not white spirit or turpentine – and wash your brushes out in water. However, never let your brushes dry with paint on them as this will ruin them. I keep mine in a 'flat' dish in water, twenty-four hours a day.

Since acrylic colour can be used opaquely or transparently, you can use an oil painting technique or a watercolour technique, so it is extremely versatile. I normally use both techniques in a single painting and work with my painting upright on an easel.

OIL TECHNIQUE

For the oil painting technique, take your brush out of the water and dry it on a rag, leaving the bristles damp. Then mix the required colours on your palette. Because the brush is just damp rather than full of water, the paint isn't watered down. It will have a buttery 'oil paint' consistency and be opaque when you brush it on to the canvas. The thicker the paint, the more opaque it will be and so it will cover other paint.

WATERCOLOUR TECHNIQUE

The main difference is that you use a lot of water to mix your paint (just as in normal watercolour painting). If you are using only a watercolour technique, have your paper at an angle and, as with traditional watercolour, don't use any white paint or this will make the colours opaque.

The scene I painted for television

In order to demonstrate the differences between these two techniques, I used the oil technique for my first painting of the television series while June worked in the watercolour technique. We painted the same subject – the pretty village of Caherdaniel – from slightly different viewpoints. Compare my painting, right, with June's painting on page 23.

I was fascinated by the brightly-painted brickwork of the houses. I wasn't concerned with the hill in the background, it was the colour of the buildings, the green fields and the trees in the village that inspired me.

I started at the top of the painting and worked down the fields, the foreground tree areas, the road and the buildings with a first coat (underpainting). For this I used the paint thin and watery. The small trees at the top of the painting were then put in and more definition was worked into the houses, road and trees.

Finally, I put in the signpost, the suggestion of cars, the telegraph pole and the two people.

Caherdaniel. Primed Waterford 300 lb Rough, 25 x 30 cm (10 x 12 in)

The painting spot I chose was
further up the hill than June's

▶ The suggestion of the two cars and the people were painted in the finishing stages. When I was painting this on television, I put in two figures and then, without thinking, painted the telegraph pole over them! Naturally, I painted two more

▶ Notice how my left to right brush strokes help to give the impression of fir trees. I painted the red of the house first before I painted the trees over the top

▲ These trees look like soldiers standing in a row – their uniformity helps to balance the picture against all the indistinct greenery behind the house. Notice how the brush strokes were worked outwards from the trunk. This helped to give shape and form

▼ After painting in the solid mass of greens for these trees, I painted the trunks and branches over the top. I then added some warm grey in places to suggest the road just showing through. I kept the edge of the house crisp and this helped to make the house look stronger

▶ The background fields were painted thinly with watery paint. The fir tree trunks and branches were painted over the background. Thicker paint was then worked over the trees to give more definition

June saw the same scene quite differently to me. Choosing a slightly lower viewpoint, she was inspired by the road that came down the hillside and led to the yellow building. This building was The Blind Piper Bar.

June decided to do an upright (portrait shape) painting to help her composition. After she had drawn it first with a 2B pencil, she started painting from the top, working down and using plenty of watery paint. Notice how the white paper was left unpainted for the cottages. As I said before, no white paint is used with a watercolour technique.

She then worked down to the bottom of the road, leaving all the buildings unpainted. When this was dry, she worked the distant trees and hedges and put the roofs and windows on the cottages. The yellow building and roofs and the chimneys behind were painted next, and then the foreground. Finally, June painted in the signpost in the foreground.

▲ The nearest cottage was painted in the same way as the furthest one, but June was more careful with its shape and that of the nearby trees, in order to establish the middle distance

▲ White paper was left to portray the distant cottages and this area was painted round very freely. The distant trees were just blobs of paint – this helped to keep them in the distance

▲ The eye is led to the yellow building and this, together with the adjoining trees, has been painted with more form and detail to make the building stand away from the hill

The Blind Piper Bar. Bockingford, 38 x 28 cm (15 x 11 in)

THE COLOURS JUNE USED

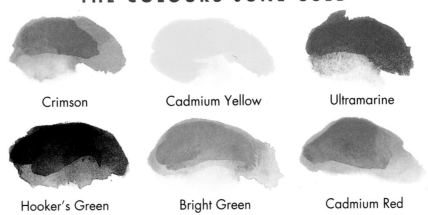

Crimson   Cadmium Yellow   Ultramarine

Hooker's Green   Bright Green   Cadmium Red

SCALE AND COLOUR

Two very important lessons are explained in this programme: scale and colour. We were very lucky where we were staying in Derrynane – there were mountains nearby which were ideal for showing scale on television.

SHOWING SCALE

Scale helps the viewer to understand a painting. For example, if you create a close-up painting of small pebbles on a beach with nothing else in the picture to show scale, it is difficult to know whether they are very small pebbles, large stones or even boulders. However, if there is also a crabshell or a cockleshell in your picture, you will know immediately that they aren't boulders.

Scale is important, especially when you are working indoors from memory or imagination. That is why it is essential to work outdoors as much as possible and to learn from nature. Observe carefully and use whatever means you can to create scale in your painting.

The simple demonstrations showing scale that I did for the television programme are reproduced on the opposite page. For the first one, I drew two identical mounds within rectangles. At that stage, the mounds could have been anything. I was going to make one of them a hill and the other a mountain but they needed scale to give them size. So I drew a house at the top of the first mound, which immediately made it into a hill. Next, I drew a very small house near the base of the second mound, making this mound into a mountain.

For my second demonstration, I drew two trees the same size as each other. I then drew a fence at

the side of the first one and a smaller fence at the side of the second one. Since we accept that most fences are similar in height, this gives the illusion that the second tree is larger.

Of course, nature doesn't always provide you with an obvious object to show scale. In that case, you may need to help it a little. For example, if you are painting a river with nothing on its banks – you often find this in estuaries with mud flats – painting in a sea bird, an old tyre that has been used for a fishing boat fender, a broken oar or a signpost in the mud will help to give your painting scale.

Scale is very important when you are painting a large panoramic view and my painting on page 48 is a good example of this. For that programme, we were at Ladies' View in Killarney, looking for a painting spot. We found one that was good for the cameras and in particular for the sound man, who was pleased that it was away from the road and the noise of traffic. However, I wasn't very happy as there was nothing in the foreground to lend scale. Eventually, we found a view where I had some trees in the foreground to show scale and this helped to create the illusion of the vast distance beyond.

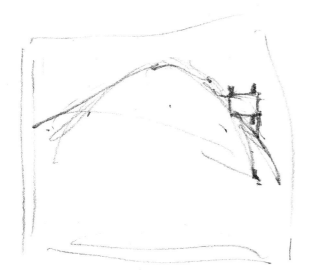

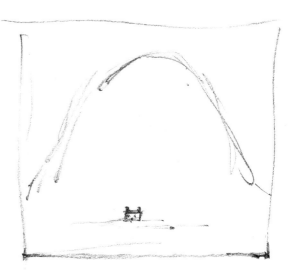

▲ By drawing a cottage on the top of the left-hand mound and a very small cottage at the foot of the right-hand one, I have shown two different

examples of scale. The first mound has become a small hill and the other mound has become a very large hill or mountain

▼ A fence was drawn against the left-hand tree to show scale. By drawing a smaller fence in my second example, the right-hand tree appears

larger. When working outside, always look around for suitable objects that could help to portray scale in your painting

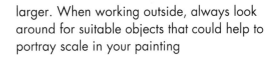

COLOUR MIXING

If you haven't painted before, it may seem impossible to mix each of the hundreds of colours that surround us. Here are four very important things to remember that will make colour mixing much easier for you.

1   You don't have to paint the exact colour you see. For example, if you are painting a blue boat, it doesn't matter if your blue is a little too green or too bright. It is the colour harmony of the whole painting that is important. This doesn't mean that you shouldn't try to get the correct colour – just don't get too involved with this, or you will start to lose concentration and inspiration for the 'whole' painting.

2   There are only three primary colours: red, yellow and blue, and you can mix any colour from just these colours. Of course, there are different hues of red, yellow and blue to help you get the exact colour you are mixing, but I use the same three primary colours most of the time. These are Ultramarine, Cadmium Yellow and Crimson. You can use ready-mixed greens, purples, oranges and so on to help you, but I suggest you start with just three primaries as you will learn to mix colours more quickly this way. I don't use black; instead I mix a 'black' colour from these primary colours.

3   When you are mixing colours, particularly from the three primaries, it is very important that the first colour you put on to your palette is the predominant colour you want to create. For example, if you want a yellowish-orange, you should put yellow on your palette and mix a smaller amount of red into it. If you put red onto your palette first and mix yellow into it, you will get a reddish-orange and, by the time you have mixed enough yellow into the red to make a yellowish-orange, you will have mixed far more paint than you need, got frustrated and wasted time. Time is not paramount, of course, but when you are working outside you are fighting the elements. Of course, if you can work quickly, it is always a bonus!

4   There are two ways of making acrylic colours lighter or paler. You can mix white paint with your colours, or simply add water to make the paint transparent. This makes the paint lighter as it does with watercolour.

On the opposite page I have used three primary colours and created other colours from them. Mixing colours can be rather frustrating at first but it can also be very enjoyable. Everyone can learn and it will become second nature to you the more you practise. In fact, most students surprise themselves. So don't think of this as a lesson, but as an exciting adventure! You will experience a wonderful feeling of success when you are able to mix the colours you need.

▲ When mixing colour, remember to mix into the predominant colour first. For all the colour mixing examples in this book, I have mixed colours together, starting with the top colour and mixing down into the other colours. Sometimes I have also worked the bottom colours back up into these colours to help show variation

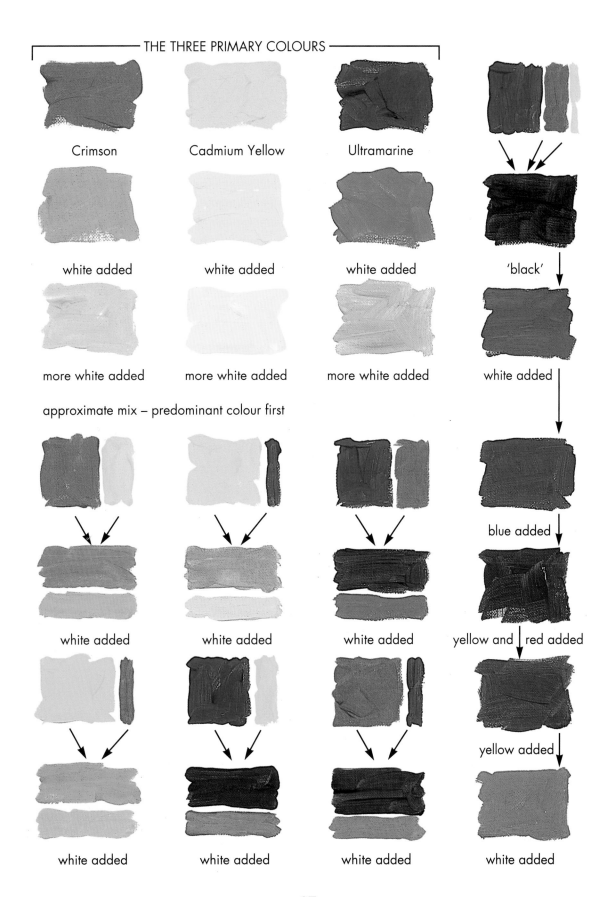

THE THREE PRIMARY COLOURS

Crimson

Cadmium Yellow

Ultramarine

white added

white added

white added

'black'

more white added

more white added

more white added

white added

approximate mix – predominant colour first

white added

white added

white added

blue added

white added

white added

white added

yellow and red added

white added

white added

white added

yellow added

white added

This is the hill that I painted from the Butter Road

When I painted the hill from the Butter Road above Derrynane, I used only my usual three primary colours: Ultramarine, Cadmium Yellow and Crimson, plus white.

The first decision I had to make was whether to paint the hill dark against a light sky, or light against a dark sky. It was very windy and the dark clouds were casting shadows constantly. One minute the hill was dark against a bright blue sky, the next it was bathed in sunshine and the sky behind it looked dark and threatening.

OBSERVATION

When you are faced with a decision like this, your choice has to be what you feel will look the best in your painting. There are no rules. When you find your scene to paint, sit for a moment and observe any changing light conditions. While you are doing this, note the different features and objects in the scene and really get the feel of it. When you start to draw and paint it, you will then feel comfortable because you know your subject.

When I first decided to paint this scene, it was quite a few minutes before I noticed the old stone house in the centre of the picture. It seemed to disappear and appear again as the light changed. However, after I had spent about ten minutes observing the scene, I felt I was familiar with it. It is at this point that you are ready to paint your scene, whatever it is.

First stage
I drew the scene with an HB pencil. The drawing was reasonably simple – the most important part was to make sure the elements of the scene were in scale. I then painted the sky, going over the top pencil line of the hill so that, when the hill was painted, the hill colour would overlap the sky and form the shape of the hill.

Halfway stage
This is the point where I really began to relax and enjoy myself. I had painted in everything except the foreground, and only detail was needed in the middle distance to bring the painting to life.

Finished stage
I put windows in the old stone cottage but was careful not to make them too dark and kept them fairly small. When I had painted in the foreground, I felt the hill could be a little darker on the left. This helped the light area of hill to the right of the stone cottage to appear more sunlit and I did this with a transparent wash.

I spent some time observing the scene before starting my painting for the television cameras

▲ *First stage*

▲ *Halfway stage*

▼ *Finished stage* From the Butter Road, above Derrynane. Cryla paper, 25 x 30 cm (10 x 12 in)

▶ I believe the cottage was still being built because there seemed to be holes for windows and the yellow areas looked like boarding. Notice how simply I painted it. My 'bend' in the telegraph pole didn't worry me! I also put the dark post in to the right of it. I had no idea what it was but it added interest to the cottage area and this is important

▶ I didn't try to make the old stone cottage more prominent than it was in reality since this would have distracted the eye from the cottage on the hill

▲ Notice how free my brush strokes were when I painted the foreground. The interest in this picture is in the middle distance and a simple foreground makes it easier for the eye to travel to the centre of interest – the cottage

▲ The dark cloud colour was painted first and the blue grey sky was worked over the top of it

▶ I didn't smooth my brush strokes out when I painted the sky. This helped to suggest moving clouds and a strong wind. The brush strokes for the rocks on the hillside were worked in the direction of the formation of the rocks

June preparing to paint for television

June also painted a hill for this programme; this one had small farm buildings at its base. The size of the buildings lent scale to the picture, making the hill appear like a small mountain. She used three different primary colours to mine for her painting: Coeruleum, Cadmium Red and Cadmium Yellow Pale.

PAINTING WITHOUT DETAIL

It was extremely windy when June was painting. This can make your hand and the surface you are working on very unsteady and in these kind of conditions it is often difficult to put careful detail into your work. June was lucky as there was no need for a lot of detail in a subject like this. If it had been a complicated scene in a town or by a harbour, it could have proved quite difficult. In such situations, the answer is usually to find a sheltered spot – providing you can still see the scene you want to paint! Alternatively, accepting the fact that you will paint a 'free' painting, rather than a tight and detailed one, is an enjoyable exercise.

It is interesting to see that, although June used different primaries, the colours in her painting are very similar to mine, except that her fields are a colder green than mine.

June started with a simple drawing using an HB pencil. Having established the top of the mountain, she drew the farm buildings and fields in the foreground.

Halfway stage
The paper is totally covered with paint, but notice how June's brush strokes have left areas of paper unpainted. This kind of 'happy accident' can happen naturally when you are painting, or you can do it intentionally. As the brush strokes follow the direction of the fall of the mountain, the unpainted areas seem to go in this direction, too. It helps to give form and shape to the painting. I think the windy conditions caused June to get that brush stroke of red paint at the top of the picture!

Finished stage
Notice how June has now toned down the red at the top of the mountain. To complete the painting, she put in the houses and then painted a dark wash over the whole of the mountain to hold it together. Finally, the three telegraph poles on the right were painted in with very pale colours. And, despite the gale-force wind, June managed to put them in with less bends than the pole I painted in my picture.

JUNE'S PRIMARY COLOURS

Cadmium Red   Cadmium Yellow Pale   Coeruleum   ▲ *Halfway stage*

▼ *Finished stage* On the road to Sneem. Primed Waterford 300 lb Rough, 28 x 30 cm (11 x 12 in)

▶ June painted the telegraph poles in with her 'Rigger' brush. After completing the painting on television, she felt they could have been a little stronger

▶ This detail shows how freely the mountain was painted. June kept the paint reasonably wet to allow the brush to move the paint smoothly and quickly over the paper

▲ Most of the farm buildings were painted in single brush strokes. Notice how the house doesn't jump out at you and neither does the cottage. It could have been very tempting to make more of the cottage, as it was the only point of interest, but when you looked at the scene it didn't leap out at you – it was just there

▶ June did the sketches on this page while she was waiting for the television crew to set up their cameras

3

FLOWERS AND FIGURES

Here I was nearly at the end of my flower painting

Because of rain, our plan to go out and paint mountains for the next television programme had to be changed quickly. The director had a good suggestion – that I should paint some flowers, and that June should paint me as I worked. I liked the idea and I thought it would make a great programme but I wasn't so sure about the subject. After all, I don't really consider myself a flower painter. However, when I had finished, I was quite surprised and pleased with the result.

PAINTING FLOWERS

I think two factors helped the picture and these are both worth noting when you are painting flowers. Firstly, I painted the shadows of the flower petals quite dark and this helped to emphasize the brightness and colour of the flowers (light against dark). Remember, when objects are light in colour, don't be afraid to give them dark shadows.

Secondly, I didn't try to paint the petals too carefully. I let them merge together and be unidentifiable in places. This helped to keep them looking soft and delicate.

It is easy to fall into the trap of trying to paint each petal exactly. It is better to look and observe where you can't make out the petals and paint them as you see them, not as you know they are. However, it is important to paint a few of them reasonably carefully because this will visually tell the story for all the other indistinct blooms and give overall character to the flower.

▶ *Halfway stage*
At this point, I had drawn the flowers quite freely
with my HB pencil, but I did a few more
carefully, especially those in the middle of the
bunch. I painted in the background, working it in
a watercolour technique, and then the leaves,
followed by the shadows on the white flowers.

▶ *Finished stage*
The shadows for the yellow flowers were put in
next, then I added the white and yellow petals
with thick paint. I painted the flower centres and
put more darks and lights in the leaves and
blooms. Some buds were painted over the leaves
and finally a shadow was painted on the wall.

Primed Waterford 300 lb Rough,
28 x 38 cm (11 x 15 in)

IMPORTANT COLOUR MIXES

**The white flowers
in shadow**
White, Ultramarine, Crimson
and Cadmium Yellow Pale

**The yellow flowers
in shadow**
Cadmium Yellow Pale, Crimson,
Ultramarine and White

The leaves
Hooker's Green, Bright Green,
Cadmium Yellow Pale, Crimson,
Ultramarine and White

▶ Notice how dark the shadows are on the petals and how strong the yellow is where the light strikes them. This dark against light really helps to portray form and shape in the painting

▶ The leaves were done as brush strokes rather than by painting an outline and then filling in. This helps to give leaves a natural look. Remember, this type of painting isn't a botanical one; you simply want to give an impression of the flowers

▲ These petals were painted very freely to keep them looking soft and delicate

▲ The petals on these flowers were worked very carefully and I gave a more positive shape to some blooms. This helps the viewer to understand the ones that have been painted more freely and indistinctly. I used thick, juicy paint for the 'white' of some of the petals

▶ I painted over the leaves with my No. 6 sable brush to add the flower buds. I then added some highlights to the buds using the same brush

SKETCHING PEOPLE

The main problem with painting people is that they seldom keep the same pose for very long! June often paints the holiday-makers sunning themselves on our local beach in Devon and she says they never stop moving. However, when she painted me for this programme, she felt reasonably in control. After all, while I was busy working at my easel, I couldn't move very far!

She used a 2B pencil on cartridge paper to draw some preliminary pencil sketches to get her brain and hand co-ordinating. This is very important when drawing people although, naturally, you may not have time to do this in some circumstances.

When doing her sketches, June started with the head and worked down the body to the feet. In a drawing like this, don't be too precise with your pencil lines. You will find that, within reason, the more lines you draw, the more movement and life you will give your figure. Don't think about rubbing any pencil lines out unless they are completely wrong and distracting to your drawing.

PENCIL AND WASH

When June had completed her drawing of me, she added a final touch by using a watercolour technique to add acrylic washes over the pencil. First, she painted washes over the face, hands, red shirt sleeves, blue waistcoat, jeans and easel. At this stage, there was no light or shade in the picture. Then, using just one colour mix for all the shadows, June painted these in. This was done very freely, but only after she had carefully observed how and where the shadows fell.

▶ 2B pencil on cartridge drawing paper
(actual size)

42

Cartridge paper (actual size)

IMPORTANT COLOUR MIXES

The sleeves
Cadmium Yellow and
Cadmium Red

**The waistcoat
and trousers**
Ultramarine and Crimson

The shadows
Ultramarine, Crimson and
Yellow Ochre

PANORAMIC LANDSCAPE

For this programme we went to Ladies' View in Killarney. The view was breathtaking and, with the shimmering lakes and the sun lighting up the distant landscape beyond the mountains, I felt really inspired. But one should never rush in and paint without thinking. As I said earlier, always relax and look at the scene until you can make sense of it and understand it.

OBSERVING THE SCENE

With a view like this, there is a great deal to take in. I spent at least half-an-hour walking around looking for a painting spot and then observing it. During this period, some areas were in shadow while others were in bright sunlight and these were constantly changing. I therefore had to decide where to paint shadow and sunlight in the scene. Now I feel that perhaps I should have painted the distant mountain shadows a little more blue, to make them recede a little more.

The rocks, boulders and trees in the foreground help to show scale, which is very important in such a panoramic landscape. The trees and boulders provide a good starting point from which the eye can travel through the picture.

If, when confronted with a view like this, you feel it is too vast for you, just paint a small section of it. Find a part of the scene that inspires you. June preferred some smaller areas as she looked round, and decided not to do the whole scene. All artists are individual and, to some, a view like the one I chose might be frightening – or uninteresting. To others, it would be like painting Utopia. Paint what you like and what inspires you – Ladies' View really inspired me!

▲ Working for the television cameras against the panoramic background of Ladies' View

▼ At this stage, I was hoping it wouldn't rain before I finished the painting. Luckily, it didn't!

▶ *Halfway stage*

At this point, I had painted the fields in the distance after drawing the scene with an HB pencil. I concentrated on the main contour lines, groups of trees and water area and didn't try to put in any detail with the pencil.

▶ *Finished stage*

Because acrylic paint dries quickly, I was able to go back over areas already painted and work in the detail where and when I wanted. It really helps with a subject like this. Remember, once you have decided where to place your shadows and sunlit areas, try to keep to these throughout your painting.

Ladies' View. Primed Waterford 300 lb Rough, 28 x 38 cm (11 x 15 in)

IMPORTANT COLOUR MIXES

The dark mountains
Raw Sienna, Ultramarine, Bright Green, Crimson and White

The greens of the trees
Bright Green, Cadmium Yellow, Ultramarine, Crimson and White

The foreground grass
Raw Sienna, Cadmium Yellow, White, Crimson and Ultramarine

▶ Much more detail was visible in the distance than I have suggested. In a painting, always keep distant objects simple or they will come forward in the picture

▶ There is quite a lot of detail on these two trees in order to make them appear in the foreground and give scale to the rest of the painting. The rocks also help to give scale. I used a dry brush technique for the spring leaves and my 'Rigger' brush for the trunks and branches. When you want thin lines, using more water with your paint allows the paint to run out of the brush

▲ I was very careful to let plenty of 'blue water' show behind these trees. This also helped to create distance. I painted some blue water back into the trees, where I felt the painting needed it

▲ I worked my brush strokes freely for the mountains but let some of the strokes form the shapes of rocks

▶ Notice how the dried grasses have been painted – they were done with up and down strokes and the marks left by the brush help to create the grassy effect. Just above the large rock, I painted a tree with a small trunk. Above that tree, I painted a light-green one against a dark background. I did these both very carefully because they were important to show scale

June was inspired by the green spire of this church against the purplish-blue mountain in the background, and the way the sun was casting strong shadows all around.

Unfortunately, by the time we were set up for filming, the sun had gone in and the scene became a little flat. However, the subject was still a good one. The lovely green of the ornate spire was still a prominent feature, silhouetted against the mountain and the sky.

PAINTING A SIMPLE SCENE

It is just as important to spend time considering how you are going to paint a simple subject like this as it is with a panoramic view. You must still look for objects to show scale and the chimney pot provides it here. Always find objects that are light against dark, or dark against light, to show form and shape. The spire is an example of this. The sun was no longer shining but June put a soft shadow on the chimney stack and spire to help to give form. The mountain was painted in shadow with a lovely 'distant blue' colour. If it had been bathed in sunlight, it would have become confused with the roof colours and wouldn't have stayed in the background.

Notice how simply June painted the slatted part of the spire. It would have been so easy to have worked this too much, as it was the only

June was almost hidden by the long grass when she painted the church for television!

decorative feature in the painting, but this is just enough for the eye to go directly to it. The composition is good, since the spire rests happily in the top third area (see page 52 for more about composition). June also varied the main roof colours to make it more interesting.

June couldn't resist sketching me at Ladies' View. Cartridge paper, 9 x 20 cm (3½ x 8 in)

Ladies' View. Cryla paper, 15 x 20 cm (6 x 8 in)

IMPORTANT COLOUR MIXES

The mountain
White, Ultramarine
and Crimson

The church spire
Bright Green, Ultramarine,
Crimson and White

The foreground grass
White, Yellow Ochre, Crimson
and Hooker's Green

SKETCHING OUTSIDE

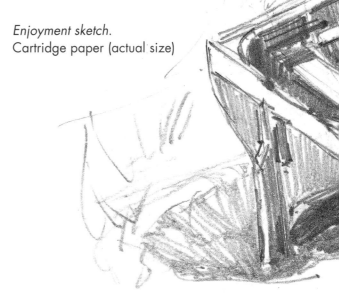

Enjoyment sketch.
Cartridge paper (actual size)

In this programme June and I spent the day sketching at Derrynane Bay. When you are sketching outside, although it is important to familiarize yourself with the area, once you see something that interests you, sketch it. It doesn't matter what subject matter you choose – but it is important that you have been inspired! I put sketching into these three categories:

1 Information sketch A drawing or painting made purely to record information or detail, which can be used later at home to paint from. I usually use my cartridge sketchbook for information sketches and find that I can put in as much information as I want just with a pencil.

2 Atmosphere sketch This is usually painted rather than drawn (since paint is better for capturing atmosphere than pencil). An atmosphere sketch doesn't have to contain a lot of detail but should enable you to remember the mood of a scene. I normally do this type of work using my Acrylic Travelling Studio.

3 Enjoyment sketch A sketch drawn or painted for the sheer pleasure of doing it and for no other reason!

Sketches can be as large or as small as you wish – there are no set rules about size. And remember that a sketch – no matter how big or how small – is still a work of art and can be framed and hung alongside any 'finished' painting. Some of John Constable's sketches were very small but many people prefer them to his larger finished paintings.

COMPOSITION

I could write a whole book about composition and design but this basic rule will help you when you are out working. If you divide your paper into thirds across and down (see my first illustration, right), any of the four points where the lines cross are considered to be natural places for your centre of interest. In the second illustration, the centre of interest is the church spire.

If you are in any doubt, use this principle and you will always have a reasonable composition. Your painting will sit happily on the paper and nothing will worry or distract the onlooker. Of course, rules can be broken, sometimes with fantastic results, and nature often provides us with the perfect composition. But, in the end, the design decision is up to you and, as you gain experience, you will find that good composition will soon become second nature to you.

▲ Divide your paper into thirds across and down. Any point at which these lines cross is an acceptable place to position your centre of interest and make a good composition

▲ I have positioned the church tower as the centre of interest in this picture. This example has the same composition as June's church on page 51

The weather was glorious on the day that June and I were filmed sketching on the beach. I wandered around looking for a painting spot for about half an hour and when I saw this scene from the rocks, with the hills in the background, I simply had to sketch it.

I drew the sketch first with an HB pencil and then started painting the sky. I continued down the painting, finishing with the highlights of the waves. This was achieved by adding thick white paint to represent foam.

STARTING A SKETCH

It isn't always necessary to start at the top of a painting and work down, especially when you are sketching. It depends on the subject and how you see it. I often start a sketch in the middle of the paper with something that inspires me, then work outwards from it until I fill the page.

While I was working, a few people walked across the beach. Because I hadn't painted the beach yet, I wasn't ready to put them in but, in case I didn't see any more people, I marked them in on the picture in pencil. When I painted the figures in later, this helped to lend scale to the beach, as well as giving life to it.

I wish now that I had painted the furthest beach darker or lighter in tone than the long beach with the people on it – it would have

The beach scene I painted for television

helped give more distance. I did put a brush stroke of lighter yellow just to the right of the dark fence at the top edge of the beach but I don't feel it was enough. But I never alter a sketch I have done outdoors when I get back because any alterations would have to be done from memory, and the object of a sketch done on location is to draw or paint what you see.

IMPORTANT COLOUR MIXES

The mountain
White, Raw Sienna,
Ultramarine and Crimson

The beach
White, Raw Sienna, Cadmium
Yellow and Crimson

The sea
White, Ultramarine, Crimson
and Bright Green

▶ Halfway stage

After painting in the sky and the hills, I didn't smooth out my brush strokes. In fact, I didn't work over this area again except to put a little more detail into the fence at the top of the beach. You can see where I marked in the size of the figures on the beach.

▼ Finished stage

Notice how simply the two figures were painted. If I had tried to put any detail into them, they would not have stayed in the distance. Remember to paint only what you can see.

Derrynane Bay. Cryla paper, 15 x 20 cm (6 x 8 in)

Here I am busy painting the fishing boat

BOATS AND WATER

I couldn't resist painting this fishing boat either! But I must admit I did put more work into it than I had intended. I became so involved that I worked a little too much on detail; in fact, I fiddled – but I like the result! It wasn't only the boat that inspired me. The cottage on the hill, bathed in sunlight, was breathtaking against the dark green of the boat in the foreground.

Firstly, I drew a pencil line across the paper to establish the water level. Then I drew the cottage and the boat. You will find that boats, even when they are moored up, will turn and move about. But they will always keep coming back to the same position. Once you have started sketching a boat at a particular angle, don't try to change your drawing if it moves. Just wait until it comes back, then continue with your sketch.

I painted the hill and cottage in the same way as the beach sketch on page 55, keeping things simple. The two posts to the left of the cottage are markers for the entrance to the harbour and these were put in with single brush stokes.

It was hard to make out the stern against the side of the hull, so I exaggerated this a little by painting the hull lighter and the stern darker. This gave dimension to the boat. I painted the water with short horizontal brush strokes, making them larger (by pressing harder on the brush) as they got to the bottom of the paper. This gave a feeling of perspective and the impression of movement on the water. There was no reflection from the boat and so I decided to put one in to help give a better illusion of water. I did this with single brush strokes.

When looking at the finished sketch later, I saw that the horizontal strut at the stern of the boat should have been nearly as high as the cabin roof. I shouldn't have missed this – but I'll blame the presence of the television cameras this time!

A harbour we visited but didn't film.
Cartridge paper, 17 x15 cm (7 x 6 in)

Fishing boat. Cryla paper, 15 x 20 cm (6 x 8 in)

IMPORTANT COLOUR MIXES

The hills
White, Raw Sienna, Crimson,
Cadmium Yellow and Bright Green

The sea
White, Ultramarine, Crimson
and Bright Green

The boat
Bright Green, Ultramarine,
Crimson and White

While I was painting for this programme, June had seen some lovely Sea Pinks growing out of crevices in the rocks and she decided they would be perfect for her first sketch.

PAINTING WHAT YOU SEE

When you are working outdoors, it is important to paint what you see and work in any way you feel will get the impression you are aiming for. Don't feel too bound by the normal techniques of painting. This particularly applies when you are out sketching, and the flower sketch June did is very typical of working outdoors. Without being consciously aware of the way she was working, she used a watercolour technique for the background and opaque colours for the flowers. June did this because she found it a natural way to paint the subject.

As you gain experience you will become used to certain ways of handling your brushes, colour mixing, the best way to make grass look like grass and so on. But sometimes your painting subject will dictate how you paint it. When this happens, don't be afraid to experiment. You will

The Sea Pinks June painted for television

find yourself working in ways you haven't tried before and gaining even more experience. Also, your painting will look more natural as a result.

June did very little drawing before she started painting since pencil lines are only a rough guide when doing a sketch like this. The most important things to establish were the dark shadow lines on the rock and the general shape of the group of flowers.

She then painted the background using a watercolour technique, leaving unpainted paper for the main blooms. When this was dry, June painted in the leaves with thin paint. She didn't try to paint these carefully or individually, but her brush strokes always followed the way they were growing.

The pink flowers were painted with thicker opaque paint. Then the dark shadows behind them were put on using very watery paint and, finally, June painted some darks on the leaves and pink highlights on the flowers. The rock was much darker behind the flowers, but June had seen a lot of pink colour in the rock itself and decided to keep the whole sketch predominantly pink in colour.

A moment to reflect in between shooting

Sea Pinks. Primed Waterford watercolour paper 300 lb, 15 x 20 cm (6 x 8 in)

IMPORTANT COLOUR MIXES

The flowers and the shadows
Crimson, White, Ultramarine and Cadmium Yellow

June's little warm-up sketch.
Cartridge paper, 9 x 10 cm (3½ x 4 in)

USING YOUR MEMORY

June was inspired by the colour of the sea and particularly by the spray coming over the rocks on the beach for the picture on the opposite page. The water was quite shallow where the rocks were and by the time the cameras were set up and June had started painting, the tide had gone further out and the spray was minimal. Before filming, June had been observing the way the spray came over the rocks, so she was able to paint this from memory. The lesson to learn here is that when you are inspired by a moving subject, start sketching there and then, or you could be too late. June had no choice and had to wait until we were ready to start filming.

If you do paint by the sea, it's worth remembering that, if you are working on a flat sandy beach, the tide will move over the beach very quickly. If the beach has a steep slope down to the water, the tide will come up or down the beach much more slowly.

June established the sea level first, then drew in the distant hills and, finally, the foreground rocks. The hills were painted leaving brush strokes showing to suggest the form of the hills. The rocks were painted very dark as they were silhouetted. It also helped to make the sea look brighter (light against dark).

June painted in the sea with horizontal brush strokes, changing the colours and tones subtly to give movement. The spray was painted with the brush strokes worked in the direction that the spray was moving and she used thicker paint for this. As June was finishing the sketch, it started to rain heavily and so it had to be completed in a hurry. Later that evening, when she looked at the picture, she felt she might have put something in to show scale – perhaps a sea bird on the foreground rocks – if she'd had the time. But she decided against adding anything to the sketch. As I said earlier, when you do a sketch outside, don't be tempted to add to it or take anything out when you get back home.

Sketches like the ones June and I did for this programme should take about 30 or 40 minutes. If you take longer, you're fiddling – as I did when painting the boat on page 57!

A quick pencil sketch on the beach. Cartridge paper, 12 x 20 cm (5 x 8 in)

Derrynane Bay. Primed Waterford watercolour paper, 15 x 20 cm (6 x 8 in)

IMPORTANT COLOUR MIXES

The hills and the rocks
Hooker's Green, Crimson, Yellow Ochre,
Ultramarine and White

The sea
Coeruleum, Ultramarine, Bright Green,
Crimson and White

6

COMPARING MEDIUMS

When we went to Doulus Head near Caherciveen to film this programme for television, it was decided that June would work using watercolours and I would paint in acrylics using a watercolour technique. We could then show the difference between the two mediums. June chose the subject – a farm cottage – and decided to paint it close-up, sitting in a nearby field. In contrast, I decided to paint the same cottage as a distant view.

ACRYLIC AND WATERCOLOUR

The main difference between these two mediums is that, once it is dry, acrylic paint isn't soluble in water. You can paint a transparent wash with it, let this dry, and then paint another wash over the top without affecting the first one. In watercolour, subsequent washes can pick up colour from previous ones.

Of course, when you are painting in watercolour, the ability to 'move' colours which have already dried and merge other colours into them is a great help and a traditional way of using that medium. However, with acrylics, you can use washes to build up depth and strength into your colours without the possibility of picking up the dry colour underneath, as in my example, above right.

When I painted the distant view, opposite, I did quite a detailed drawing before I started painting, then began at the top using Bright Green as my main colour. I left the buildings and sheep unpainted at that stage. I used three washes for the beach area (incidentally, the sea was covering most of my beach before I had

The same strength of acrylic wash was painted six times to build up colour

finished!) but notice how I left quite a lot of white paper showing to give the impression of light on the rocks. I painted a roof on the cottage and windows and a door, leaving the rest of it unpainted paper. Finally, the outbuildings and sheep were painted in. I wonder now if I should have left some of the sheep as unpainted paper.

Although I was using a watercolour technique, my acrylic colours didn't merge together in the same way that they would have done if I had been working with watercolour. I think this makes the colours appear brighter.

The rocks and stones on the beach were much easier to paint as there was no risk of pulling up any dry paint. In fact, I could have worked over and over the painting without fear of making it 'muddy', as can happen when using watercolour. But I decided that, since the cottage was the centre of interest, the foreground had been worked enough.

▲ My distant view of the cottage

▼ *Doulus Head.* Watercolour technique on Waterford watercolour paper, 28 x 38 cm (11 x 15 in)

▶ You can see here how transparent acrylic paint can be. Look at the trees to see where my washes have gone over each other. I painted the cottage windows and door very simply

▶ The stones and rocks on the beach were painted with one wash, first changing the colours as I worked. When this was dry, I painted darker shapes in some areas to suggest rocks. Finally, I painted some darker shadows to define a few of the rocks. The large brown one is a good example of this. It was made up of three separate washes

◄ I left unpainted shapes for the sheep on the white paper when I painted the grass. Later I added a little colour. I feel I could have left one or two more sheep as unpainted paper. I made the farm look three-dimensional by painting a shadow on the right-hand side (dark against light)

◄ Notice how pale I painted the fence. It is so easy to make something like this too strong so that it jumps out of a painting at the viewer. If you can only just see an object in the distance, paint what you see and not what you know is there

USING WATERCOLOUR

Now it was June's turn to paint the same cottage, but this time from a different viewpoint and working in watercolour instead of acrylic. She didn't have my problem of the tide coming in when she painted her scene, but she did have the sheep in her field to contend with!

June had used an acrylic watercolour technique in Programme 1. When she did her painting of the cottage, right, she felt the main difference when using watercolour was that the paint ran down the paper more quickly and easily, and this meant it was not as easy to control as acrylic paint.

When we had finished both our paintings, we compared them. Accepting that different artists paint differently, they both looked like watercolours. My picture was slightly more defined than June's, but that's the way we paint.

So why use acrylic colours to paint in a watercolour technique when the results seem so similar? Well, you may like the way you can build up washes with acrylics and work using plenty of water – you may even find it easier to work with than watercolour! Certainly, this technique adds another dimension to acrylic painting, particularly as you can combine watercolour and oil techniques in one painting, as well as using them separately. In the gallery section, you will see paintings that June and I have done using both these techniques.

The cottage from June's painting spot

Halfway stage
June started with the sky and worked down the hill but left an unpainted edge between the sky and hill to stop the washes running together. She left the house and telegraph poles as unpainted paper but suggested the windows with simple brush strokes.

Finished stage
The roof and trees were painted in next. The tree trunks were important shapes for the eye to understand and to enhance the painting, so June did these carefully with her 'Rigger' brush. She didn't touch the foreground again but she did paint a darker wash over the hillside to push this feature back in the painting.

June's pencil sketch of a nearby hedgerow. Cartridge paper, 8 x 17 cm (3 x 7 in)

▲ *Halfway stage*

▼ *Finished stage Doulus Head.* Watercolour technique on Bockingford 200lb, 17 x 28 cm (7 x 11 in)

▶ June left an edge of unpainted paper to stop the sky running into the hill, although she did allow it to happen in one or two places

▶ The doors and windows were painted in very freely with a No. 6 sable brush. Look at the lump at the bottom of the telegraph pole. Seen in isolation this could concern the viewer, but when seen as part of the whole painting, you don't even notice it. Don't worry too much about things like this

◀ June had to paint the tree trunks carefully – but without too much detail – to show shape and form. I think these have worked well in the painting

JUNE'S WATERCOLOURS

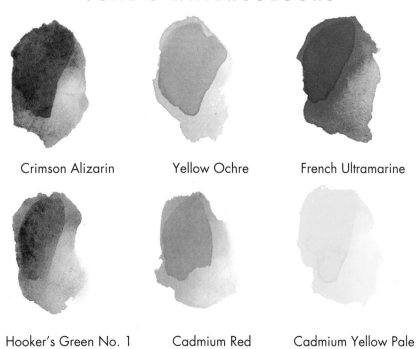

Crimson Alizarin   Yellow Ochre   French Ultramarine

Hooker's Green No. 1   Cadmium Red   Cadmium Yellow Pale

7

PAINTING PEOPLE

When David, our producer, suggested that we should paint inside the Blue Bull Bar at Sneem, June and I saw this as a fantastic challenge. It wasn't going to be easy, with customers coming and going the whole time – not to mention finding room inside this busy Irish pub for the two of us, an easel, two cameras, lighting and sound equipment and the television crew! Before we started working under camera, we sketched with a 2B pencil in our sketchbooks to get into the mood. The sketches on this page are mine and the one opposite is June's.

Painting inside the Blue Bull

The man with the pipe. 12 x 10 cm (5 x 4 in)

The accordionist. 12 x 12 cm (5 x 5 in)

June was filmed while she sat at the bar sketching the customers

One of June's warm-up pencil sketches. 15 x 15 cm (6 x 6 in)

June working in her sketchbook, apparently not worried at all by the pub noise and activity!

PAINTING ON BROWN PAPER

To show the versatility of acrylic paint, I used brown wrapping paper to paint on for this programme. I had bought this from the local ironmonger's shop.

I did the preliminary pencil sketch, below, in the Blue Bull the night before filming to show David, the producer, where I could work from while still leaving just enough room for the cameras. When I did this sketch, I started with the three people who are grouped together. This was lucky because, just as I finished them, they moved away. I then concentrated on drawing in the background.

When I did my painting, right, the next day, there was plenty of distraction, lots of background noise and my view was constantly being blotted out by people. However, once I got used to all the interruptions, I really enjoyed myself. Once again, my subjects wouldn't keep still! The left-hand group in my painting did stay put until about halfway through the painting, which was good. Incidentally, I found the brown paper perfect to work on. I expected it to cockle, but it hardly did at all.

▲ *The bar at the Blue Bull, Sneem.*
Brown wrapping paper, 28 x 38 cm (11 x 15 in)

▼ I did this sketch the night before we filmed the television programme. Because people move, it is best to draw them first and then the surroundings.
Cartridge paper, 20 x 28 cm (8 x 11 in)

▶ I used a 3B pencil to draw on the brown paper. This man's face was painted very simply. He does look sad – perhaps it was the tune he was playing! Notice how much brown paper I left showing. This helped to unify and give movement to the painting. It was a good background colour to work on for this kind of subject. In fact, I also decided to leave brown paper unpainted for the floor

COLOUR MIXING ON BROWN PAPER

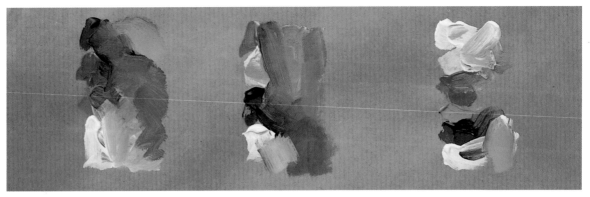

The mens' jackets
Ultramarine, Crimson, Raw Sienna and White

The browns
Crimson, Cadmium Yellow, Ultramarine and White

Gold highlights and green bottles
White, Cadmium Yellow, Crimson, Bright Green and Ultramarine

▲ I haven't put any detail on this man's face; it doesn't need it. Notice how my brush strokes follow the fall of his clothes. I could afford to work a little slower than when I was drawing the scene, because by now I had established the position of the people

▲ I painted the bottles and jars on the shelves (shown here and opposite) very quickly. I just wanted to give an impression of them

PEOPLE IN GROUPS

When you are drawing a group of people, don't worry if one of them moves away before you have finished. They may come back and assume roughly the same position and, if they don't, someone else might fill their place who you can draw instead. Otherwise, leave them out of your group altogether, or put someone else in from another part of your setting. You need to have some experience for this. If the group or part of it goes altogether, there is only one answer – start again with another group.

One way to make things easier is to go out with your own friends and ask them to stay together while you draw them. You may have to buy a few drinks, but it's worth it! Just sit quietly in a corner with your 2B pencil and sketchbook and practise. You will soon find your pencil starts working faster and this is very important.

Once you have drawn the figures in your picture with pencil, you will be ready to start painting (remember, the background is constant). If your characters move, you can recall the colour of their clothing and you should also have taken notes as you drew them of the tonal areas. For example, you would notice that the light green jacket was showing up against the dark background, or that the trousers of the 'jolly' man blended into the dark of the floor, and so on. You need a certain amount of courage and experience to go out painting like this. But it's a challenge and very exciting. And it needn't be a pub – it could be any indoor gathering.

You can see how much drawing June did for her sketch of the man at the bar, opposite. He had offered to pose for June but this didn't stop him moving and turning round to chat to his friends. But at least he stayed in the same place for most of the time! Notice how many pencil lines there are for just one shape – the man's back, for example. June's pencil has gone over that part with five or six lines. You will find you do this automatically once you gain experience; it is an unconscious way of feeling the shape and movement of your subject. June used an acrylic watercolour technique for this painting, as she did in the sketch of me on page 43.

June sketched the same group of people that I painted on brown paper.
Cartridge paper, 10 x 10 cm (4 x 4 in)

Cartridge paper
(actual size)

SIMPLIFYING A SCENE

When I first looked at the village of Sneem from the hill, the view really excited me. A lot of beginners avoid a subject like this, thinking it is too complicated to paint. The answer is to simplify things and to paint an impression of the scene. Try to capture the atmosphere that inspired you to have a go.

SHAPES AND COLOURS

When simplifying a complicated scene, accept the fact that you are not trying to paint objects like houses, trees or cars in detail, but as shapes and colours.

When you paint, concentrate on your subject – don't let your mind wander! For example, if you are painting a delicate cloud, think about the soft texture of the cloud as you paint it. Then your brain will tell your brush to work delicately over the paper. If you are thinking about rocks as you paint your clouds, they will probably end up looking very heavy and more like stones!

Letting your brain tell your brush what object it is painting is very important when simplifying objects. Even when you are suggesting something very simple in your painting, you will create a feeling of that image, especially when it is seen as part of a whole painting. Look at the close-up details of my painting on pages 82 and 83. Out of context, it is difficult to understand what has been painted in some areas.

Always remember to make something in, or near, your centre of interest more defined. This helps to make the scene understandable to the viewer. I did this with the row of houses which line the main road in my picture.

My view of Sneem from the hill

Halfway stage
I stood up to sketch, holding my sketchpad so I couldn't get too involved with drawing detail. However, I positioned important areas like the mountain slope, houses and main street carefully. I then painted the mountain thinly, keeping the detail of the trees and far houses to an absolute minimum. I used a Cryla Series C25 brush for the rooftops (each brush stroke was a rooftop) and added some green for fields and trees. I left most of the houses as white paper at this stage; others I painted soft pastel colours using the same brush as I did for the roofs. You can see how my mind was conditioned to simplifying everything.

Finished stage
The rest of the painting was done in the same free way as the first stage but I did add a little detail to the row of houses on the main road. Incidentally, I love working detail in a painting, so I had to keep reminding myself of the type of painting I was doing!

▲ *Halfway stage*

▼ *Finished stage Sneem.* Cryla paper, 25 x 35 cm (10 x 14 in)

▶ You can see the freedom of the brush strokes and lack of detail. Notice how simply the chimney pots have been painted. These were done with single brush strokes

IMPORTANT COLOUR MIXES

The mountain
Raw Sienna, Cadmium Yellow, Crimson, Bright Green, Ultramarine and White

The rooftops
White, Ultramarine, Crimson and Cadmium Yellow

The greens
Bright Green, Cadmium Yellow, White, Crimson and Ultramarine

▲ You may find the two close-up details shown above fairly difficult to identify in the finished painting because they were painted very freely. But, in context with the whole of the painting, they make sense

▲ This section shows the centre of interest where I worked a little more carefully and with more detail to give stability to the painting

▶ In contrast, look at how freely my brush strokes were worked in this part of the painting

PAINTING A SMALL PICTURE

Like me, June had been inspired by the bright colours of the houses in Sneem. In fact, from her painting position, she could see more of them. June had decided to work lower down the hill from a totally different viewpoint. She decided to do a small painting on paper measuring 15 x 20 cm (6 x 8 in) to show how this can be done with a large, complicated scene.

June needed to simplify things even more than I had done in my larger painting and so she worked very freely. The brush strokes are very obvious and these give tremendous movement and strength to such a small painting.

When she was preparing to paint, a cloud shadow fell over the mountains and the sun was on the buildings. This is how June decided to paint the scene. Remember, with clouds moving all the time, a scene – especially when it is a vast landscape – will change constantly. So you have to make a decision and stick to it. The mountains were painted thinly for the first coat. The houses in front of the mountain were all worked with a Cryla Series C25 brush, nearly all with single brushstrokes. June used thicker paint to do this.

The foreground trees were painted with strong brush strokes. As the trees were in shadow, this helped to give an impression of sunlight on the village and field (dark against light).

June painting the village of Sneem

When June had finished, she wondered if she had painted this picture a little too loosely. I don't think so. It is a perfect example of how all artists see things differently. Normally, June doesn't work as freely as she did that day, especially at this size. But it's always a good exercise to try something different. One of the great lessons you learn from simplifying a scene is to stop fiddling and, if you approach it in the right spirit, it should be a very enjoyable experience. Why don't you have a go? It's easier than you think!

June did this quick pencil sketch while I was being filmed. Cartridge paper, 7 x 17 cm (3 x 7 in)

Sneem. Cryla paper, 15 x 20 cm (6 x 8 in)

IMPORTANT COLOUR MIXES

The mountains
Yellow Ochre, Crimson,
Ultramarine, White and
Bright Green

The greens
Bright Green, White,
Hooker's Green, Yellow Ochre,
Crimson and Ultramarine

The village
Crimson, Cadmium Yellow,
White, Bright Green,
Coeruleum and Ultramarine

Clearing up. Acrylic watercolour
technique on Waterford 300 lb
Rough, 50 x 80 cm (20 x 30 in)

GALLERY

▲ *Sunlight on Shaldon, Devon.* Acrylic on Cryla paper, 23 x 28 cm (9 x 11 in)

▲ *Low tide, Shaldon, Devon.* Acrylic on Cryla paper, 15 x 20 cm (6 x 8 in)

▲ *Exmouth from the Exe.* Acrylic on Cryla paper, 15 x 20 cm (6 x 8 in)

▲ *Warm spring day, Shaldon, Devon.* Acrylic on Cryla paper, 26 x 37 cm (10½ x 14½ in)

Exmouth Harbour. Acrylic on canvas,
40 x 50 cm (16 x 20 in)

ALWYN CRAWSHAW

▲ *Tulips.* Acrylic watercolour technique on Bockingford 200 lb Rough, 38 x 28 cm (15 x 11 in)

▲ *Shaldon beach.* Acrylic watercolour technique on Bockingford 200 lb Rough,
25 x 38 cm (10 x 15 in)

▲ *From Blackslade Water, Dartmoor.* Acrylic on primed Waterford 300 lb Rough,
25 x 30 cm (10 x 12 in)

Sunflowers. Acrylic watercolour technique on Whatman 200 lb Rough, 28 x 38 cm (11 x 15 in)